Dismantled Secrets

Dismantled Secrets

Poems by Maxianne Berger

WOLSAK
& WYNN

Cover photo: Doug Williams
Author photo: Doug Williams
Cover design: Rachel Rosen
Typeset in Adobe Garamond, printed in Canada by The Coach House Printing Company, Toronto, Ontario

Poems from this collection have appeared in the following magazines and anthologies: *American Tanka, Carve, Chili Verde Review, dANDelion, Gusts, The North American Review, Pouèt-cafëe!, War, Literature & the Arts, An International Journal of the Humanities, and Wooden Basement Newsletter; ars poetica, Australian Poetry Collaboration, Bywords, Fluent Ascension, The Hamilton Stone Review,* and *Queer Poetry I: Mixed Nuts; Ash Moon Anthology* (Modern English Tanka Press, forthcoming), *Fuchsia Snowflakes* (Wooden Basement Press, 2001), *Haiku Canada Holographic Anthology* (Haiku Canada, 2004), *In Fine Form: The Anthology of Canadian Form Poetry* (Polestar, 2005), *The Paradelle: An Anthology* (Red Hen Press, 2005), *Sun Through the Blinds: Montreal Haiku Today* (Shoreline, 2003), *These Silent Rooms* (Haiku Canada: 2003) and *Tulip Haiku* (Shoreline, 2004)

The publisher gratefully acknowledges the support of The Canada Council for the Arts, the Ontario Arts Council and The Department of Canadian Heritage for their financial assistance.

Wolsak and Wynn Publishers Ltd
69 Hughson Street North, Ste. 102
Hamilton, ON
Canada L8R 1G5

Berger, Maxianne, 1949-
Dismantled secrets / Maxianne Berger.

Poems.
ISBN 978-1-894987-24-0

I. Title.

PS8553.E673D58 2008 C811'.54 C2008-901376-X

1 Prevailing winds

2 Between maroon and indigo

3 The woman in the carpet

4 The opera of her life

5 Beautiful homes of the horsy set

6 The ABCs of desire

in memory of
Linda Ross
(1948-2000)

beside her grave
an apple tree – its leaves
cling to the branches

Advice to one bursting with a secret that mustn't be told

Arrange a bowl of ripe peaches on your kitchen table.
Tell your secret to each one. Your secret is safe
for the silent peach is virtuous, both heart and tongue.

Take a walk in the woods, far from your home.
Find a tree with a knothole too small for a bird
and whisper your secret, then fill it with mud.

Tell the grass grown wild on your front lawn.
Take out your mower and mow each blade down
before the wind gets wind of the words and blows.

Take a hot shower. That jasmine-scented soap? Let it
be your confidant. Lather your skin with the words
then rinse, and watch them sputter down the drain.

Tell the rain. Tell the rain that falls on the city streets.
The raindrops might well tell the sidewalks but
the gist will get lost in the splatter and splash.

Tell one who is mad – your deranged cousin – whose
sharp gestures punctuate discordant verbal fugues.
The mad one will tell all, but none will believe a word.

Tell a poet, for a poet dismantles secrets, hides the pieces
in schemes and tropes. What you want no one to hear,
the poet will surely reveal, but none will believe a word.

1 Prevailing winds

one year later
the grass completely grown in
over her grave

Prevailing winds

It's a question of measure,
clarinet notes

held over a beat too long
during the season of empty streets.

Only clothes
remain hanging on the branches:

a single argyle sock; a red felt boater
(someone's taken a bite out of the brim);

a tweed overcoat, its pockets
lined with holes.

And the dog
jumps up and down like a pogo stick

barking at flappy sleeves as if,
like a conductor's arms,

baton in hand, they'd mark
the rhythm of prevailing winds.

palliative care
windowsill full of flowers
adrift in the scent
she spends her days counting
the minutes till her next pill

Scout leader

be prepared to answer questions
the Scouting Manual doesn't address

bears? drug dealers? venereal disease?
be prepared for leukemia – a pernicious strain –
to waylay one of your spirited charges

be prepared to watch him shrivel into shadow

be prepared to find his 15-year-old sister
wailing in your arms – his gregarious mother
silent with her twisted handkerchief

be prepared to camp out in palliative care –
your share of a death watch: graveyard shift

be prepared for morphine drips,
for beeping monitors; for doctors
– Lord knows they tried –
who press a firm hand to your shoulder
when there's nothing left to say

be prepared to curse

be prepared to curse God
and be prepared to pray
the boy will hold on long enough
his grandma who lives overseas
can make it in for one final hug

be prepared for nurses in tears

be prepared when his father requests a eulogy –
practice saying it without sobbing

be prepared for a half-sized coffin

be prepared for a funeral
for a troupe of boys in uniform
who'll follow your every lead

be prepared to show them how
a real man weeps

After this second winter of chemotherapy

Another April –
the Foothills of the Rockies
still hooded with snow –
a whole valley away yet
they fill her picture window

The sunlit mountains –
she smiles at them. Sometimes
she closes her eyes.
Then at night, while she's asleep,
the mountain winds come knocking.

Night winds shake the house:
like poltergeists they rattle
whatever rattles.
Mornings, she finds her paintings
hang, still, but at odd angles

"How do they do it?"

early morning coffee
tops
the hospital cafeteria
fuck

while his father
bottoms
lies in coronary care
get fucked

he addresses
verses like
his mother's wary query
me

in meted words
do both and
when
everybody sucks

she asks
he says
about gay sex
about gay sex

Intensive Care Ward
through his bedside window
icicles
heavy under the eaves
ready to drop

After midnight, intensive care ward

The hand he holds
already cold

moments after
the final breath,

one ear pressed
to his father's chest,

he listens
as the silences

between beats
grow longer;

listens till
his father's

pacemaker

Lavender and hedgehogs

Words of comfort flicker and blur
in the dictionary of grief. Today, we turn

its alphabetic pages, reading
hampered by damp and hollow eyes

that mark us: who loved and were loved,
who cared and were there and are here.

And after sorrow it will happen
that comfort will catch us

unawares – from a bolt of cotton
rolling out its fine floral spray

to the muted glint served in the bowl
of some tiny silver spoon.

Comfort might come fragile
with the whimsy of a paper doll,

or steady in the calligraphic
brush strokes of faïence.

Some day comfort will guide us
through the door to another room,

will hold our hand, briefly,
to the doorknob itself.

And we'll hear comfort when the air
we breathe   each spring   tells us

honeysuckle, lilac, hyacinth,
lavender

Tombstone

It always hurts when they carve in the first name
little pieces of myself – chips and dust on the floor
more, even, than when they cut me from the quarry
honed me to the right size and polished my face –
it hurts to be beautiful – but numbers, letters, scrolls:
a ritual tattoo – and the memory of pain filling
days and nights for years... till the second one's
final numbers were added. Now the pain returns
only when the young ones pay a visit – sure
they bring flowers – and fewer tears each year –
but one day they'll stop coming, leave me forever
alone with sun, snow, sleet, rain – the night terrors,
the muffled sobbing of my younger neighbours
newly grounded in nearby rows – this waiting

2 Between maroon and indigo

black against black
the train before dawn
growing smaller

the ferry's foghorn
morning mist on the river
no horizon

Somewhere between maroon and indigo

A gargoyle sputters, uncouples from its drainpipe,
cobbles its desperate way across the flagstones.
An owl swivels, ears marauding beyond its gaze;
treble flickering, the hourglass fills with moths.
Violets, breathless from the moon's touch,
wonder where nightmares go to rejoice.

A cross gargoyle uncouples pipe tones. The way it flags,
drains a sputter from the cobbles, it's desperate.
With flickering ears, marauding moths treble.
An hour swivels beyond glass; the owl fills its gaze.
Breathless nightmares go to the moon
where violets rejoice from wonder's touch.

Moths rejoice across the moon's ears where
a gargoyle swivels with nightmares. The hour
fills pipes; its glass violets drain; its cobbles
go from breathless gaze to flickering sputter.
Way beyond the flagstones, a marauding treble
uncouples from wonder, its owl-touch desperate.

Housekeeping

They reached the edge of the world
  on that rainy day
    they'd been saving for

all those years
  they'd gunnysacked
    gripes and bickering

over whose turn it was to turn
  the conjugal bed towards the moon
    on any given night,

if quibbles on the forest floor
  were better swept
    in fall or spring,

or whether the bowl that spilled
  regret might've been stirred
    more caringly.

And in that tempest at the brink,
  shivering and vertiginous, they couldn't
    come to terms with leaving

their stockpile of annoyances
  out in the rain: would
    they be cleansed,

or slide, lathered in mud,
  unceremoniously
    over the edge?

Passion lies

Passion lies
rumpled in the laundry hamper

stained with lust &
reeking of sex

wash after wash, remains
rumpled and inside out

because when they sorted
through life's gritty issues

they argued incessantly
as to passion's being

light
or dark.

Rumours

Along distant walls, bookcases gather
titles of message and memory. Tacit mirrors
ponder as knickknacks strain to hear

the bedrooms juxtaposing diffusely above.
Even those wretched backyards are listening!

Why don't large egos rejoice a willing mattress?
Pillows cosy up to the most vibrant requests,
feathers satisfy the happiest space, and you –

seeking praise in your own reminiscence –
simply dismiss the whole jubilant weekend.

Where would sweet old biddies ever marry?
Geraniums gesture devoutly over this.

The womb

The womb:
remember its rhythm?
our mind shaped by
overlaps?

Remember its rhythm?
The folding over of a veil
overlaps
our eyes' open sea.

The folding over of a veil –
its hint of
our eyes: open sea;
wayward; inevitable beast.

Its hint of
swallowed chagrin; the odd,
wayward, inevitable beast
beyond limits.

Swallowed chagrin (the odd
colour) shifts
beyond limits,
changes our overflow seeds.

Colour shifts
our mind. Shaped by
changes, our overflow seeds
the womb.

plundered from Gregory Betts's
"Plunderverse: A Cartographic Manifesto"

The magician

late late into the starless night
he sobs
against her bolted door

cloudburst
no umbrella
up his sleeve

top hat floats in the gutter
soggy rabbit
hops away

Broken off

There's that angel with only one wing.
Walking. There. Between the tombstones.
Yesterday I saw her (as I always do, alone),
gathering dandelions in the Public Gardens.

No, that's not a limp, it's a list:
weight unbalanced on her shoulders. See
the stump? On the left side? They say
losing that wing dislodged her heart.

She spends days staring at the sky,
her face runneled with white salt lines,
knowing she'll never again see heaven.

Nights, she lies on the side of her loss,
spreads her one wing over her body,
nestles into its stone-cold feathers.

February

Snow falls
on fallen snow

filling
the footprints

left
by your leaving

Notes to Beattie Elmer's Sonnet VIII, "After she left him, he"

[1]That summer, Margrit (Elmer) Caldicott implored Bertram Caldicott to emboss griffins on wallpaper rollers.

[2]Recently discovered notebooks reveal that only in 1992 did Stephan Carrerro notice the menacing gargoyle poised over the doorway to his grandparents' brownstone though he did his homework there every day after school except for grade seven. The entry describes "green-painted knuckle stubs where the right foot's talons have fallen away."

[3]The allusion is to a haiku written that same winter:

high winds, freezing rain –
makes no difference to a dog –
hey! a walk's a walk

[4]In a related paper on the topic of infixed expletives, Ross concludes that all native speakers perform similarly – as in *un-fucking-believable* and *inde-goddamned-pendent.*

[5]By then it was too late: Margrit Elmer had quit school, pawned her pearl necklace and purchased weed killer to rid the front lawn of those daisies her mother so abhorred.

[6]Elmer's niece. A Trans-B wormed into Mary's software, leaving her more than a little bit pregnant. Her gynecologist harrumphed it, but Mary, insistent, gave his name to thirteen contacts in her address book. They all gave birth to nerds.

[7]Elmer's sister Margrit's in-laws' country neighbours kept their garden pond stocked with rainbow trout and flounder. The coroner assumed that Bertram contracted pneumonia when he neglected to remove the ermine coat he wore all summer.

[8]The irony to Margrit's being brained by falling debris whilst cycling to work has escaped many previous analysts.

[9]The fuel economy on Stephan's rover was so poor "5 bucks couldn't get it across the bridge." Elmer underscores the cumulative cost through deft alliteration of V-words.

[10] These last lines, scrawled in red on the manuscript, though reprinted in anthologies, are attributed by most experts to the poet's nephew Lazarus, sole curator of her texts. No final couplet ever surfaced in her hand, and the marginal belief of respected researchers is that Beattie Elmer rejected any envoi because, spiritually, she and Stephan never parted.

3 The woman in the carpet

fire-gutted house –
on the doorstep
this morning's paper

schoolmate, himself a child,
shot her
their beautiful daughter

The woman in the carpet
(After Makhmalbaf's *Gabbeh*)

when they rolled open
the knotted wool carpet
they found a woman
her blue dress unraveling
brown hair long and loose
tangled with winds of the steppe
matted with the silt of river banks

the hand-spun fibers
dyed in flowers and berries of the fields
feel coarse as the far hills
slate peaks against a rippled sky

her eyes drawn open
appear to focus
but she never could see
the black-hooded rider
approaching behind
muddied boots smudging
the grey mare's flanks

as he bears down on her

her mouth contorts

there she remains

always out of reach

Theft

Eyelet curtains tremble:
a wingèd creature scrambles

over the sill, somehow unremarked.
Callused feet cross worn carpet

feathered fingers rifle dreams where
curled together, two beings share

a single pair of silk pajamas.
Scarlet only murmurs in this dark,
quiet as confetti in their hair.

A H

When he carved his initials in six
thin strokes with the pocket knife
she'd given him for Christmas years
before, Miranda went into a trance.
Bitch, he'd whispered caressing her
face with the blade, *now they'll know*
you're mine.

This morning the doctor teased out one
hundred fifteen stitches. Miranda could feel
each one's tickle pulling through
her cheeks' still-swollen flesh.
Bitch, he'd breathed, *look who's beautiful*
now! – as he drew the thin, red letters
into her skin.

Why didn't you leave? they accused.
Leave? Miranda remembers her shoulders
pressed into corner walls, a poster
crooked over their unmade bed, her ring
fingers fused together, numbed in his
grip. Leave? Couldn't she only move
deeper in?

Trailing her fingertips over her face,
she imagines how a baseball feels –
the knife in his hand – *leave*, they accused –
bitch, bitch, Miranda babbles to herself
as, for the first time since the attack,
she manages a mirror, and the mirror
laughs.

But the hole is still not deep enough

The manuring shovel, never
 intended for such a task, creaked
each time the pigtailed girl
 scooped up another load of earth.
"Mother, when can we stop digging?"

Squinting through eyelids swollen
 blue, the woman stepped in
to fathom depth: barely to her knees.
 "The hole is still not deep
enough." She raised the axe high
 above her head and swung
all of an arc, hacking hard at the next,
 deeper, layer of rocky soil.

And daughter, pushing hair
 off her face, braids untwined
more from this night's work than
 from her father's mussing,
set again to digging, the ache of her
 arms' and shoulders' exertion
overpowering the memory of that
 jab between her legs.

Her mother attacked the earth
 again, the axe's mud-coated blade
now well-pardoned of its blood. Through
 the long night, turn by
turn, mother and daughter dug and
 dug till a racket of crows
signaled the job was done.

They dragged his body to the hole,
          flopped it over the edge; next
retrieved the head from where it
          had rolled and wedged itself,
the day before, in the pile of kindling.

          Flies dispersed.

                    They dropped it in.

These are the particles

You'll notice these particles when the ice
melts inside a plastic tumbler. In space,
those possessed by integral spin cannot

be distinguished from the ones standing
alone in the dell. Like modest wall flowers
they shrink from the music of spheres,

producing visible auroras when their orbits
cross the Earth's. Their blush shrieks as purple
as a meteor's. Scientists use a sweep magnet

that traps and holds particles which standard
filters cannot catch, in order to gather specimens
for Show & Tell. Field operators dissect them,

rearranging protons and neutrons, wanting
to create and annihilate particles that can't be
sorted, classified, or coloured inside the lines.

These carry the push and pull of gravity, slog
along the bottom of the human mind, clogging
DNA with off-key sing-song. Buildings provide

no refuge: air indoors is permeated with modified
particles as stale as smoke. Health effects include
(but are not limited to) perma-grin and premature

death. On Earth, nearly all known matter
combines protons, neutrons and electrons.
Long-lived particles known to bear grudges,

they damage spacecraft, and some say,
in a parallel universe, a red shovel
idles in a sandbox where no children play.

empty schoolyard
only a few crows pacing
near the swings
what are they waiting for?
another gunman?

Bad news paradelle

Coffee spilled all over the morning.
Coffee, spilled all over. The morning
soaked the embers of yesterday's smile.
Soaked the embers. Of yesterday's smile,
embers spilled yesterday's morning
over all the coffee, the soaked smile.

Lips thickened. Murmurs of tar-
lips, thickened murmurs of tar.
Cream curdled. In mid-pour
cream curdled; in mid-pour
murmurs pour in tar, curdled
mid-thickened cream of lips.

Floats like sulphur scum on silence.
Floats like sulphur. Scum on silence
gelid words inside. My mouth
gelid words. Inside my mouth,
silence floats gelid. Inside words
like my sulphur mouth. On scum.

In the gelid cream of silence,
morning floats over embers
like lips spilled on sulphur coffee,
over scum. All yesterday my mouth
thickened words. Inside the mid-smile,
curdled tar's soaked of murmurs.

Sweetening the lesson

Children, when very hungry,
will lick and suck honey from
wherever it is spread.

So the white slavers know
how to teach fellatio.

A BLIND EYE

Some say the story's an ancient myth
that they wove a universe in the cloth

to swaddle the goddess and while she burned
brazen in the pits of their minds they heard

the shrieks of childbirth escape her throat
but they were men they didn't know

the melting moon ladled an oozy swath
around the blue marble of Earth that turned
turned like a blind eye inertially below

4 The opera of her life

outdoor performance –
on stage with the dancers
a moth

after Beethoven
a scatter of dead leaves
& a single glove

The most proper discussion

Manic discussions juggled fancies,
concocted sunbeams, valleys, a tale.
They wanted the loquacious loop.

But venomous reviews overflowed:
"Discussions' concerns should be grandiose;
not these babbles distorted as by telephone."

Words climbed into the fearful Sciences
where a number-cruncher was staging
an exuberant production of dance and dream.

A poet tried to process the writhing form
but the interrupt twitched weirdly,
toggling between random errors of pathos.

The opera of her life

The Soprano wears a blue dress.
This is a tradition. Typically
the skirt shows signs of shredding,
the bodice, red and black stains
which under certain lighting conditions –
say a backdrop of everyday *verismo* –
seem more indigo or maroon.

When the Soprano nears the apron
to deliver her first aria, the role
calls for her to appear apprehensive
as she purses her lips
to release the gathering melody.

The Basso Profundo leaps to his feet:
as if in *solo declamato*,
his deep resonances
eclipse the song the soprano
might have sung.

They stage this opera
the same way each time:
Tenor, Bass and Baritone –
in counterpoint or polyphony –
pre-empt her every aria. Even
the chorus overwhelms
the Soprano's attempts to sing.

The finale features all soloists and chorus
for a rousing rendition of the opera's
leitmotifs. All, that is, save the
Soprano. During the coda,
stage directions leave her seated,
elbows on knees, head in hands.

At curtain call: the Soprano smiles,
breasts the customary bouquet,
and curtseying low,
dissembles her resigned coloratura
into her skirt's gathered folds.

Brava! Brava! The audience
according her a standing ovation
bless her performance.

And critics far and wide
acclaim
her silence.

In patterns of regret

rhythm shaped
  beyond where wine influences us

to explore
  deep seeds
  buried in the garden of a book

the key, however, is
  in repeated sonic babble, distortions

reflection of the world,
  the echo unveils poets
  striking out words
  built from the stick of disregard

striking out words
  the echo unveils poets'
  reflection of the world
  in repeated sonic babble: distortions

the key, however, is
  buried in the garden of a book

deep seeds
  to explore
  beyond where wine influences us

rhythm, shaped
  in patterns of regret

plundered from Gregory Betts's
"Plunderverse: A Cartographic Manifesto"

Ode to a round tuit

A poem is never finished, it is only abandoned.
—Paul Valéry

Like a Philosopher's Stone of resolve
informing a procrastinator's dream,
you provide the exalted wherewithal
to start and complete whatever chores remain
undone. Couch-potatoing with panache,
dilly-dalliers seem taken aback
when accused of sloth. "Soon," they swear,
"I'll finish when I get
a round tuit" – you, pearl of their prayers,
panacea for the indolent.

Were you square or oval, Tuit, if
you graced my home – you, the means to every
end – then dust bunnies would vanish with
those bills littering the desk, my heavy
self would slender, the basket full of mending
wouldn't overflow, and I'd phone my friend in
Paris to catch up. But finding Lapis
Philosophorum,
Elixir or Grail is far easier a task
than mining for your Unobtanium.

As to this poem which is not yet polished,
had I the tool toolissimo, I'd be inspired
to rhyme my "polished" more cleverly than "foolish"
and I'd pentameter the rhythm as required.
Oh, Tuit, elusive as time and rarer
than assiduity, I've persevered
to keep you high up on my shopping list.
The job's no matter: you're primed to do it.
So I'll revise this ode tomorrow – let's
trust I'll get around to it.

"And Oprah nixed it,"
she sniffs. Mrs. Arbuth
runs the Golf Club
book group. Between
sips of chamomile tea,
she gushes that according to
Women's Wear Daily, this
bestseller, the author's
fifth, "reincarnates
Flobbert's Madam Bovey.
Soon," she explains,
"it'll be a minor
classic of the genre."

Professor Vincent reshuffles papers and clears
his mind. "The, um, horizons of expectations set up in
the implied author," he mumbles into his notes,
"include binary oppositions between the, um,
phallologocentric archetype" – he underlines
phallologocentric with a studied snicker –
"an archetype, um, of dialectic materialism versus
the essentialist gynocentrism of the ideal reader."

Magda, the filing clerk from Medical Records,
hands the book to Ginny, the receptionist in Emerge.
"It's another one of those stories?" She's breathless
from the stairs. "This married woman? It's her diary?
She meets her lover at lunch? and he really wants her
money? Just like that other book? It had a red cover?"

"Whereas The
London Literary Review
dismissed it as 'typical
North-American
trash masquerading
as worthwhile fiction.'"

"The affective leap of faith reflects the, um, collective
unconscious and its intertextual mythemes. The novel
– um, any novel, really – is a mere commodification for
an eviscerated adjunct of, um, cultural apologetics."

"A place in the middle's a bit sticky? to read?
And close to the end? it gets hard to understand?"

"Surely Madison Avenue
would never publish
hardcover editions of
books they consider trash."

"My sister? she was reading it in the kitchen?
Marmalade got on the pages? And me, I spilled
coffee? So to see the letters? you need to squint?"

"Interpretive communities can easily recognize
the, um, heresies of its intentional fallacies."

"Anyway, this book? It's good to read on the bus?"

"The first chapter's truly
riveting. That said, I
admit I haven't managed
any further. Though I do
gather from reports
on Entertainment Tonight
there's already a bidding war
to buy the movie rights."

"Um, yes, this novel will definitely be on the exam."

The bowler

the man who posed for Magritte
returns to retrieve his bowler.

the artist sees
                only a hat
bobbling six feet above the floor

the man is tall
he has a limp
                the hat
casts no shadow

Cinéma nouvelle vague

we are a nation of umbrellas
scoping through the cracked windows of alchemy

the torturer believes himself virile and tucks
a blue knife into his right back pocket

like spies that rise from the sewer grates,
like a hymnal wisping its calligraphed notes
up from the composer's parchment

the rain continues, licking paint
under the window sash, gnawing
the clawed foot of a canopy bed

there is something grey about the monastery,
an icon's glare of disapproval

now without purpose, umbrellas close
and through rosetted windows:

a bronchiate filigree insinuates
leaden lines along the marquetry floor
leading to an altar where

a man, the last
man, lies
still

Constrained response

Flashy and feisty, furious fun, this ostensibly
Obsessive, off-the-wall opus has received
Rich recognition and the rat's reward of censure.

Constipated critics consider its comic heuristics
Hollow and hammy; harangue and ravage its
Robust rap, its rambunctious idiosyncrasies.
Ill-conceived idea, they insist, with smugness.
Startling stanzas, but a steel-souled stunt, total
Trickery when taken together. Invective
Intended to insure this *ingenious affectation*, this
Artful atrocity will achieve absolute notoriety.
Nimble nonsense! Noisome balladeering!

Balls! This bestseller's beguiling, an opulent
Oeuvre; and open-minded opinions kibosh those
Know-it-all killjoys with keen kudos for its flash

5 Beautiful Homes of the Horsy Set

just think –
buried under all this snow
tulip bulbs!

what power!
I wash my windows and
the sun shines brighter

Beautiful homes of the horsy set

She swept the Derbies clean in '96 and '98. Now three years
out to pasture after racing's most brilliant trotting career,
Ginger Witherston, silken-maned, high-spirited sorrel,
adored and doting dam of two-year-old MakeHaste,
has earned a further distinction in winning *HB*'s inaugural
Horse-Beautiful Dot-Com Stable Makeover Contest.

The five-thousand-dollar stall renovations completed
in just three days last summer were overseen
by *Horse Beautiful*'s own Martá Ezdurta, the irreverent
decoratrix and sly CEO of Charming Barns Forever.
Transforming the sleeping quarters of Ginger's delightful
gambrel-roofed Victorian couldn't have been more fun for us.

Ginger wanted a new look, fresher stalls, but not to fight
the centuries-old feel of her stable – a decision we endorsed.
To describe her colour tastes she brought out a dried-hay
arrangement of amber, ochre, and burnt sienna. The stall's
maroon wood floor, already part of that scheme, enabled
our team to focus resources on accents, ceiling and walls.

The results (page 58) marry form to function and grace.
Of particular note, the collection of shoes, saddles and bridles
compose a playful collage of leather and metal under the loft
among framed photos of Ginger wreathed in winner's laurels.
As well, a weatherboard display case beside the water trough
shows off to perfection her medals, ribbons and silver cups.

Ginger loved the effect so much we placed a matching but
slightly smaller étagère in the stall MakeHaste calls home
when away from the circuit. The gelding, not to be outdone,
has already proven the old horse saw *like mother, like son*.
Our magazine's online version posts for interested clientele
several panoramic views of work in progress on the stalls.

www.HorseBeautiful.com/Withers.html

Indoor garden, winter

A forced bulb
won't
flower twice.

Her
experience

my proverbial
black thumb

yield to this
hyacinth's
blooming
defiance

The Carnal Interlude

Beware the Carnal Interlude:
eight-limbed like an arachnid, kin
to Shakespeare's beast of two backs,
with double head plunked on two necks.

And while its hungry faces stick
together – tongue in groove, and lip
hermetically sealed to lip – though
otherwise preoccupied, its mouths
can still devour entire
Sunday afternoons.

It lusts for time and will intrude
on gardening, laundry, all that you'd
set precious hours aside to do.
How shrewdly it secures the mood
with music and solicitude!

It coos and nuzzles, wooing hard,
inducing you to be seduced.
Such subterfuge! I'm warning you:
it's got two faces; don't be fooled.

Its delicate airs change and soon
creak of bed-slat, slurp of lubed
pudenda, and cacophony of off-key
groans – rude, lewd – suck the clock
till all the hours have been used.

Your feather bed could be its lair.
Should you find one lurking there,
shoo it lest its charms lead you
to languor whence you'll linger and
ignore your chores.

And don't go thinking I'm a prude
for warning you – my main concern
is wasted time – but here's the worst
about that Carnal Interlude: it's got
no clothes – it's downright nude!

His daughter turns seventeen

"No! I hate you!"
she slams the porch door
plunks herself down
rolls a cigarette

When she was born
she was so small
his cupped hands
form a bowl

that still holds
something so fragile
he can't bring himself
to let it slip away

his voice breaks
so tiny
hands   parted
drop to his side

Stamping out stars

So much work! You might as well make pudding with the Milky Way!
I don't plan to enter heaven on a soup ladle, she says.

And she looks so tiny standing in that
gigantic long-handled stainless-steel
bowl of a spoon, knee-deep in primordial
ooze, arms folded across her aproned chest,
matter-of-fact chin thrust at the moon.

And because she says "heaven," don't assume
she believes in God The Almighty
serving up a sip of what He Hath Wrought –
it's all a metaphor for not wanting to spend
inordinate amounts of time

peeling and slicing and salting and rinsing
and basting, sautéing, pureeing and mincing
and grilling and dicing and basting and turning
and measuring, mashing, more basting and serving
and pricking and rolling and stuffing and roasting
potatoes and onions and parsley and peppers
and cranberries, mint leaves, molasses and lettuce
and raisins and garlic, tomatoes and turkey –

None of this! None
of this! She punctuates resolve
once and for all
by stamping out stars
one by one

from a perfectly rolled
layer of dough,
confectioned to yield
the most glorious crispiest
galaxies.

the snow's melted – still
my neighbour's forsythia
can't shake off winter

bright yellow blossoms cling to
branches strung with Christmas lights –

Guided tour of Wanuskewin Heritage Park

On the edge of the prairie where Opimihaw Creek
flows into the South Saskatchewan River, the First Peoples
found peace in a place that has changed very little
over thousands of years.
<www.wanuskewin.com>

sky everywhere
rainless   dirt path   dust
through brittle grasses

... this garden...

clay pots
sunk to their collars
barely leafed bare twigs

... indigenous plants...

or nothing
labels on sticks
growing out of dry earth

Indian Breadroot
Western Wild Bergamot
Slender Beard Tongue

... prior to Contact
many of them...

Giant Hyssop
Cut-Leaved Anemone
False Dandelion

... medicinal...

Low Everlasting
Dotted Blazingstar
Saskatoon

My inner self

When the inner self attains righteousness and virtue,
the external physical being invariably cultivates merit.
— the *Saman Suttam*

He who is controlled by objects loses possession of his inner self.
— Chuang Tzu

Every one rushes elsewhere and into the future, because
no one wants to face one's own inner self.
— Michel de Montaigne

Now in all of us, [. . . .] does the normal evolution of character
chiefly consist in the straightening out and unifying of the inner self.
— William James

Many even think that it is pathological to look into one's own inner
self: as a theologian once assured me, it leads to melancholia.
— Carl Jung

The inner self is also an eminently deconstructible entity in the
Derridan sense that it undermines its own claim to meaning by
rendering what is supposed to be private in a necessarily public way.
— Adam Archibald

Today my inner self is
wearing a hat, a tweed
fedora, granite/brick

Donegal tweed flecked
with magenta (but just a hint,
to give it spark);

and slipped, there, into
the tuck, the pleated tuck
of its grosgrain band

pinching the crown on
the right-hand side, two small
tufted feathers,

ostrich feathers dyed
rose Damask. And but for
the business of that

hat, its stubby brim angled
low, over her eyes, shadow not
quite obscuring

her enigmatic smile,
my inner self is wearing
nothing at all.

"All that leisure," he insists, a morning she doesn't work

Breakfast plates take care not to clatter;
rinse themselves and slip
nonchalantly into the dishwasher.

Laundry chooses up sides and tosses
a coin for first load. Calling tails,
the whites win dibs on hotter water.
Somehow, no detergent spills.
After the work-out, the cool-down rinse,
his cotton T-shirts, dizzy with spin,
shoulder themselves around plastic hangers
for chin-ups on the shower-curtain rod.

The vacuum cleaner changes its own bag,
and then simply refuses to budge
for all the carpet's coaxing. Her purse,
after its trip to the bank, doesn't want
another outing. But today even groceries
cooperate. At the corner store, a dozen eggs,
applesauce and cheddar, clamber from shelves,
pay their own bill, and march single file
along the street the two blocks home,
letting themselves in like latch-key kids.
And just as well-behaved, each item knows
its place in the fridge and puts itself away.

Refreshed, his grey pinstripe suit returns
from a sleep-over at the cleaners.
Without any help at all, the stove brings
some soup to a boil, then lets it simmer.
It's the ladle that ladles it into her bowl.

Toast spontaneously toasts, sidles around
some cheese, and glides quite independently
onto her plate. And while the countertop
wipes away crumbs, on its very own,
lunch sets itself on the kitchen table
and waits patiently for her to sit down.

On mornings like this, when she doesn't work,
why, even her poems write themselves.

Pigeon

Is this where I catch the bus
to Central Street?
Hey! Down here! By your feet!
Central Street?
Is this the right bus stop?
Why do you look so shocked?
Oh, you're wondering
about my broken wing,
it being in a sling and all –

Last Wednesday afternoon
hightailing it downtown
I flew into one of those
plate-glass windows.
Now picture this: moments before
I'm soaring through open sky
when without any warning
this damn building leaps right up
and blocks my path.
And now I can't fly
till the wing's healed.

Stupid me.
I was tipsy from some
rum cake crumbs.
Back door, Chez Paree –
their desserts are always great.
And very very laced.

Well, here's my bus.
Nice talking to you.
Tootle-oo!

6 The ABCs of desire

her low-cut dress
his raised eyebrow
their dance

testing a mattress
they laugh like a young couple
testing a mattress

Excerpts from the blog of J. Alfred Prufrock

With a bald spot in the middle of my hair –
[They will say: "How his hair is growing thin!"]
—T.S.Eliot

Maybe we should just take off
since tonight seems strung out to next month
like an OD'ed addict on a gurney;
let's take off for the town's back alleys,
the strobe-lit raves of
fitful insomnia in flop houses
and after-hours clubs lousy with boozers:
alleys that meander like a two-tongued tale
of hidden agendas
that make you seriously wonder . . .
Well don't even ask, *What the fuck's up?*
Let's just take off and see what's what.

They go to the women's room in pairs.
What do they talk about in there?

The virtual angst that trolls the web for wannababes,
the virtual bluster that trolls the bars for wannababes
sunk its claws into the cracks of night,
slunk around the trash that litters the gutters,
ripped open green garbage bags and scattered
ill-wrapped leftovers, then jumped like the devil
when it sensed the threat of McAfee's cat,
and four-O-four'ed itself in a flash.

And it'll have its day for sure
the virtual bluster that slinks in back alleys,
that trolls for wannababes;
a day for a real-life
face-to-face and everything that follows;

a day to delete and recompose,
and a day for scoring big and one for those
that slosh and spill their issues on your lap;
a day for each of us in turn
and time too for a meg of neuroses
and for a meg of indiscretions and disclosures
before we actually meet for a coffee.

They go to the women's room in pairs.
What do they talk about in there?

And it'll have its day for sure
the question *should I?* and *should I?*
The day to update my profile,
post pix without the airbrushed paunch –
(yeah, they'll Instant Message: "u c his spare tire?")
my armpits stained from the waitress's flirting at lunch
though the shirt's otherwise ironed and clean –
(in the chatroom they'll post *He's got a nice smile!*)
Should I
click into the real world?
Online it can take a while
for neuroses and disclosures to show up on the screen.

By now I'm wise to all of them, wise to all their ways –
wise from all the yawning nights, the fog-eyed three-AMs alone
I made myself the sum of login-names and passwords,
I've dialed up chicks on dial-a-friend and heard
the background beat empowering their egos on the phone.
So what am I supposed to say?

By now I'm wise to all those web sites, wise to all their ways –
websites wiling us with sex, though they change its name: say
intimacy instead of *sex*, and a gazillion gullish women
pop up fresh from the relationship recycle bin.
So where do I fit in
when I'm mere beefcake in some techie's market game?
And what am I supposed to say?

By now I'm wise to all sorts of CVs of the heart,
CVs that exaggerate, prevaricate, or lay wounds bare
(I've learned to read between the lines to find my soul mates!)
Can the décolletage of a dress
induce me to conclude the best?
CVs that lie about their age, and minimize their past.
So what am I supposed to say?
And where do I fit in?
. . . . .

Empty chairs

She really misses her boyfriend
some mornings sitting alone
with coffee in her dark kitchen
debating what she might've done.

The same mornings he sits alone
and wonders why he's so depressed
dating; what he might've done
also to get a pick-up for sex.

She wonders why she's so depressed
without this man – her mind astir
also at what he'd pick up from sex –
face to face with his empty chair.

Without any man in mind, stirring
his coffee in the dark kitchen
he faces a faceless empty chair,
really wishes he had a boyfriend.

Their hearts

Their hearts recognize the random conflagration of vocabulary.
Their hearts recognize the random conflagration of vocabulary
but we can only speak in a language not our own.
But we can only speak in a language not our own:
we can recognize in the hearts' random language their
vocabulary, not our own, but speak only of a conflagration.

It meant radical twisting to wash the language of play.
It meant radical twisting. To wash the language of play,
perhaps beyond liquor, we share the depths of histories.
Perhaps. Beyond liquor, we share the depths of histories.
Perhaps histories meant the twisting of language beyond
radical play. To wash it, we share the depths of liquor.

Fragments of voice struggle, but the music resists
fragments of voice. Struggle, but the music resists.
A myth trapped the forest. Falling in love with her cloak,
a myth trapped the forest, falling in love with her. Cloak:
cloak music with love of myth. The forest resists her
but a falling voice, trapped, fragments in the struggle.

Beyond falling, voice resists. But the cloak meant not only
a random language, but a forest of radical music. We
speak – play perhaps – with the depths of their conflagration:
we can wash it in the liquor of language, recognize
the struggle to share. Love, trapped in her own twisting
vocabulary, fragments the myth of our hearts' histories.

plundered from Gregory Betts's
"Plunderverse: A Cartographic Manifesto"

"....?"

Well yes, that bar
downtown is fine
for meeting guys.
And yes, I'm sure
the one last night
who brought you home
and said he'd phone
is Mister Right.

But if he's just
the next Don Juan
to *done you wrong*,
well, nothing's lost:
the perfect man's
no one-night stand.

My ex wife

After Robert Browning

Here's my son's room, love. I'm a weekend dad
of course. The portrait in that gilt frame? That's
his mom. Karsh himself, at my insistence,
captured the unadulterated bliss
of pregnancy. A blessèd Madonna,
don't you think? Karsh was famous for wanting
to record his subjects' deepest essence –
engineered by any means. You might guess
that he flattered her with comparisons
to great ladies who posed for his cameras
through the years; that the look of joy you see
is just a look, something drawn out when he
redressed her self-image. Women become
obese in mind, too, inside that blubber:
it was lovingly I called her "Lardo,"
but her Beluga body was hardly
Rubenesque. And don't assume her grand smile
resulted from Yours Truly's presence while
Karsh could only elicit some blank stare.
Sure, I was her biggest fan, always there
cheering her on: *Dear, you look radiant* –
and cracking jokes: *Hey, tub, let's trade you in*
for a svelter model . . . Like you, honey!
Have I mentioned you are The Most Stunning
woman in my life to date? But listen:
that happy-face of hers was a fixture,
indiscriminate. So my adoring
compliments and fancy gifts earned no more
gratitude than when some crack-assed plumber
snaked a sink. She seemed more thrilled by our son's
crayon-scribbled card than by the bracelet
I ordered from Cartier last Mother's Day.

The former Mrs, she lacks discernment.
I dressed her in designer clothes, perfect
for cocktails, my business soirées, or just
plain lunch with friends. But the truth is, I dressed
her closets with those clothes 'cause she prefers
plebeian jeans. And the husband deserves
lots more recognition than a char, right?
Furs! Jewels! The ex got it all from me. Yet
floors, scrubbed and waxed, lit up the same warm eyes
with the same warm thanks! For drudge, as for my
favours! A simple soul of simple tastes,
she hasn't bothered suing for more – makes
do with the one million I gave her – plus
child support. She's got this tiny pink house,
garden full of vegetables – Nature Girl,
straw hat, weeding away her manicure!
Oh, and she's a poetess! Enough said?
Enough said. Come, let's look at my etchings,
here, in the den. And when we're ready – mmmm!? –
my piece de resistance in the bedroom:
an original Kama Sutra print.
Would you believe I managed to outbid
two museums to nab that masterpiece?
You'll soon see, love, we share the same, fine taste.

Exploring

An alcove of stucco and fieldstone;
and two hopefuls who've just joined forces,
we've chanced into this room of sorts
bare of furniture save for the lone

question mark on the hard oak floor.
As question marks go, this one holds
a certain promise: large and electric
blue with a fine satin finish; its aura,

pulsing like a pheromone, projects
the whole length of the curved wall.
The dot, we decide, will serve us
for a pillow; and later we can uncurl

the helix, draw it like a blanket
taut to our chins. And the embedded
question? Perhaps the answer lies
encoded somewhere in the afterglow.

She gets to know him better

Ppffhhh! ? A low-pitched fart?
Not him, sipping wine, beside her on the porch
but somewhere out on the river, off to the right.

"A whale!" He jumps to his feet. "Look!"
He points to one of many waves and ripples
indistinguishable in early evening sun.

"Must be the ferry," she says, unconvinced.
Ppffhhh! And dorsal fin, black body, fluke,
not a hundred yards off the quay. And gone.

He trains his binoculars at one more flash of tail,
then hands them to her. "Focus with your left eye
and turn this wheel till the image comes clear."

He knows which shadow in dark waters
hides its whale. She hasn't learned to read
the surface, let alone what lies beneath.

"Never mind." She gives them back, satisfied,
for now, to catch whatever happens to emerge.
Something expected. Something still a surprise.

Because of the blues

Because every drainpipe
deserves a gargoyle

Because rain puddles
welcome schoolgirls
joy! joy! joy in rubber boots

Because when chrysanthemums bloom
geraniums stay defiantly red
their clay pots
staunch on the windowsill

Because of fresh laundered sheets
stretched taut across a bed
skin on skin fingers lips
the intricate weavings of limbs

Because some mornings the sun
rises so quickly the moon
slips like silver on satin
into the sky's blue pocket

Because wine's red residue
has glazed the bowls of two glasses
with the taste of night

Because crunchy is a food group

Because a high-ride unicycle's
quite insane as urban transportation

Because you are a clown a cinephile
sportif a husky dude a lover
of books of cookies of
driving-deep-to-the-body groove

But most of all because I
can't help being a fool
this poem's for you

wild clover
overruns
the bedclothes
kiss me again
we'll gather a bouquet

The ABCs of desire

Apprehensive about any activity
        approaching ardour, asexual
angels – assuming angels are
        asexual, and almost all appear
ambiguously anti-androgynous...
        Anyway, angels are aghast at
adolescents' amorous amusements,
        and advocate against
bawdy bacchanals by belittling
        benign bedroom behaviour.

But boys beguiled by bare breasts
        become bolder, boners bulge
bigger, because clerics can't create
        confirmed celibates, can't
control carnal cravings. Challenged
        devils, defiant, don't desist;
debauchery's devotees don't deny
        desire, despite every effing
ecclesiastic's effort for
        forbidding fornication.

Fortunately, generous gods
        grant humans healthy insight,
independent judgment – knowing
        kittenish, laugh-lightened,
legitimate love might never
        otherwise occur.

Only one obstacle:
        ordained orators object
obstreperously, pounding pulpits,
        pushing passionate "purity":

Pious people, prythee! Pursue
propriety's quiet restraints, reject
sin, sublimate sex so that
those terribly unspeakable
venereal vices won't win.

Well, what's wrong with wantonness?
        Whosoever waxes
worthiest, wastes words.
        Women want whoopee.
Women who wouldn't wench.
        Women who wouldn't whore.
Wholesome women.
        Women who want willies with warmth
would wed. Women who want
        warmth without willies would wed
women. While women who want
        wild writhing, without
withdrawal, would welcome warriors
        wielding well-woodied
x-rated yardsticks. Yes, you youngsters,
        your yang, your zest!

Notes & Acknowledgments

I am grateful to all the editors who have included versions of some of these poems in their magazines, anthologies and webzines.

"Housekeeping," which appears in Bywords, was selected by GoodReports.Net as 23/04/07 poem of the week.

"Excerpts from the Blog of J. Alfred Prufrock" and "My Ex Wife" are palimpsests of the poems referred to below the titles. "Beautiful Homes of the Horsy Set" was triggered by the misreading of 'Horse' for 'House' in "House Beautiful." The first three stanzas are structured to follow the syntax of the opening paragraphs of the article "Room Makeover, Step-by-Step" by Jim Willhite. "The Womb," "In Patterns of Regret" and "Their Hearts" are composed of words 'plundered' from "Plunderverse: A Cartographic Manifesto" by Gregory Betts (Poetics Canada 5, summer 2005; poetics.ca/poetics05/05betts.html)

The epigraph by Adam Archibald to "My Inner Self" is used with permission.

Special thanks to Noelle Allen, Marja Jacobs and Simone Saunders of Wolsak and Wynn for their incredibly supportive and encouraging midwifery.

To my fellow poets in the Monday morning group and to those on the Crewrt-L writing list, for their general support and consultation; to Peter Kom and to Sharon H. Nelson whose chance comments inspired several of these poems; and to Doug Williams who patiently listened to so many versions, my deepest thanks.